KNOW YOUR SPORT

Hockey

Clive Gifford

SALFORD LIBRARIES	
SP0529147X	
Bertrams	18.05.08
J796.355	£12.99

Franklin Watts Australia
Hachette Children's Books
Level 17/207 Kent Street
Sydney NSW 2000

© Franklin Watts 2008
Series editor: Jeremy Smith
Art director: Jonathan Hair

Series designed and created for Franklin Watts by Painted Fish Ltd.
Designer: Rita Storey
Editor: Nicola Edwards
Photography: Tudor Photography, Banbury

A CIP catalogue record for this book is available from the British Library.

Dewey classification: 796.355
ISBN: 978 0 7496 7837 1
Printed in China

Franklin Watts is a division of Hachette Children's Books, an Hachette Livre UK company.

Note: At the time of going to press, the statistics and player profiles in this book were up to date. However, due to some players' active participation in the sport, it is possible that some of these may now be out of date.

Picture credits

©2004 AFP/Getty Images p15, 16 and 24;
©1999 Getty Images p21.

Cover images: Tudor Photography, Banbury.

All photos posed by models.
Thanks to Nicholas Best, Matthew Bull, Emily Court, Rosie Gladden, Mollie Hart, Harry Loxton, Bati Mupasi, Hayley Nunneley and Samantha Humphreys.

The Publisher would like to thank Bloxham School and Banbury Hockey Club for all their help.

Taking part in sport is a fun way to get fit, but like any form of physical exercise it has an element of risk, particularly if you are unfit, overweight or suffer from any medical conditions. It is advisable to consult a healthcare professional before beginning any programme of exercise.

Contents

What is Hockey?	**6**
The Pitch and Umpires	**8**
Kit and Training	**10**
The Push and the Hit	**12**
Passing and Receiving	**14**
Moving with the Ball	**16**
Attacking	**18**
Shooting and Defending	**20**
Intercepting and Tackling	**22**
The Penalty Corner	**24**
Goalkeeping and Penalties	**26**
Statistics and Records	**28**
Glossary	**29**
Index	**30**

What is Hockey?

Hockey is an action-packed eleven-a-side team ball sport where each team aims to score goals. It is sometimes called field hockey to distinguish it from the six-a-side game of ice hockey. Played on a large pitch made of grass or artificial materials, hockey is a dynamic, incredibly skilful sport.

The Game

A full hockey game is made up of two halves of 35 minutes. Each half is started with a pushback from the centre spot when a player pushes the ball back to a team-mate. A pushback is also used to restart the game after a goal is scored. Each team has a goalkeeper who is allowed to handle, kick and stop the ball with his or her body. The players in the rest of the team must only touch the ball with their curved hockey stick and only then on its open, flat side (see page 11). Using their stick skilfully, players run with the ball and pass it to team-mates with the aim of moving up the pitch and into an area known as the shooting circle. Inside that circle, they can take a shot on goal. The team who scores the most goals wins the game.

Top Tournaments

Hockey is played in leagues and other competitions by hundreds of thousands of players in more than 100 countries worldwide. Hockey for men first appeared at the Olympic Games in 1908 and, apart from in 1912 and 1924, has featured at every

This attacker has flicked the ball over the diving goalkeeper and towards the net. Hockey games are won by teams scoring goals. The ball has to completely cross the goal line between the two goal posts and the crossbar.

6

What is Hockey?

Hockey's History

The name hockey comes from an old French word *hoquet*, meaning a shepherd's crook. Hockey-like games with curved sticks and balls were played by the Ancient Egyptians, Greeks, Persians and ancient cultures in Asia. Hockey began to develop into the sport we know today during the 19th century. The first recognized club was the Blackheath Football and Hockey Club, founded in London in 1861, and 31 years later the first full set of international rules were published. In 1924, the International Hockey Federation (FIH) was formed which now runs the sport and organizes its top tournaments.

◀ One player runs and controls the ball whilst shielding it from an opponent. Hockey requires high levels of skill and athleticism.

Olympics since. Women's hockey arrived at the Olympics in 1980 and has become a popular event. World Cup tournaments for men and women first appeared in the 1970s and are now held every four years, whilst the Champions Trophy, the third most important competition, is now held every year.

Starting to Play

Young players starting out may play mini hockey, a scaled down version of the game played by seven players a side across half a regular hockey pitch. Mini hockey games usually last 24 minutes, split into two 12-minute halves. There are also different skills games and schemes run in different countries, such as Stix Skills in England and Minkey, a game for under 9s, in Australia.

Olympic Champions

Between 1928 and 1956, the Indian men's team won every Olympic Games hockey tournament, six in total.

The Pitch and Umpires

Versions of hockey are played indoors but the full game is played outside on a large rectangular pitch. Pitches always used to be made of grass, but increasingly artificial turf pitches are used, which allow the ball to run faster and bounce less.

The Pitch and Goals

The pitch measures 91.4 metres long by 58 metres wide. It has a series of markings including a halfway line, from the middle of which pushbacks are taken to start and restart the game. At the ends of the pitch, positioned in the middle of the backline, are two goals, each 3.66m wide by 2.14m high. The goals, which are at least 0.9m deep, have a 460-millimetre-high backboard running around their inside. A semi-circular area known as the shooting or striking circle or 'D' is marked at each end of the pitch. Players can only score from shots taken inside these areas.

- Between the posts of the goal, the backline is called the goal line.
- Sideline
- Halfway line
- Striking circle or D
- Backline runs across ends of both pitch.
- Penalty spot is 6.4m from the goal line.

In and Out of Play

The hockey ball is in play until it crosses one of the edges of the pitch. If it crosses the sideline, then a player from the team that did not touch it last takes a sideline hit-in. This can be a push or hit shot (see pages 12–13) with the ball placed just behind the sideline from around the same place it left the pitch. If the ball goes out of play across the backline and the attacking team touched it last, a 15m hit is taken 15m from the backline by the defending

◄ This player takes a long corner for his team. He stands on the backline with the ball placed no more than 5m from the corner flag.

8

The Pitch and Umpires

Hit-in from sideline

Goal scored

Time stopped

The umpire communicates his or her decisions to players, spectators and the other umpire by using signals.

team. If a defender touched the ball last before it went out, the umpire has to judge whether it was intended to take the ball out of play. If it was, then a penalty corner is awarded, otherwise a long corner is taken by the attacking team (see pages 24–25).

The Umpires

In charge of each game are two umpires who uphold the rules of hockey, judge on how to restart the game when the ball goes out of play and decide whether fouls or rule-breaking have occurred. Many minor infringements, such as the ball accidentally hitting a player's feet in the middle of the pitch, result in the umpire awarding a free hit. This is hockey's equivalent of the football free kick, with the opponents retreating 5m from the ball.

Three Card System

The umpires have three cards to warn and penalize players for fouls. Fouls can range from arguing with the umpire or handling the ball to pushing, tripping or kicking an opponent. The green card is shown as an official warning to a player. If a more serious offence occurs, the umpire will show a yellow card and the player will have to leave the pitch for five minutes. This is sometimes known as a sin-binning. A red card is awarded for very serious foul play such as fighting or repeated fouls. The player has to leave the pitch and the team has to continue with one player short for the rest of the game.

The player in the red shirt is performing a foul by pulling the shirt of her opponent. Her stick is almost performing another foul by hooking around her opponent's stick. Players are not allowed to interfere with an opponent's stick in any way.

9

Kit and Training

Eleven players form a team on a hockey pitch, although a team can have up to five substitutes on the bench waiting to exchange places. The eleven-person team is divided up into one goalkeeper and ten outfield players, who usually play in a formation of lines of defenders, midfielders and forwards (attackers). All eleven players hold and use a hockey stick and wear certain clothing.

Playing Kit

The outfield players' kit is simple with shirts and shorts for boys and sports skirts for girls. Long socks are worn over special hockey shinguards which offer more protection than those worn in football. Coloured mouthguards are used (so that umpires can clearly see them being worn) just in case the ball rears up towards a player's face. Some players also choose to wear padded hockey gloves to protect the backs of their hands from knocks on the knuckles. Players used to wear studded hockey boots, but with pitches increasingly being made of artificial turf, they now wear turf boots which have small pimples on the sole to provide grip. Hockey players cover many kilometres in a full game, so their footwear must fit well and be comfortable.

Goalkeeper's Kit

With a hockey ball sometimes travelling towards goal at speeds of over 120 kilometres an hour, it is no surprise that a hockey goalkeeper's kit is extensive. It is made up of heavily padded protectors for their bodies, a helmet with full face mask, foam-filled leg pad or guards and padded kickers over their boots. Sometimes, shots have to be stopped and saved with their hands so goalkeepers also wear heavily-padded gloves.

Ball and Stick

A hockey ball is hard, usually white, and about the same size as a cricket ball. With the exception of the goalkeeper, players

Helmet
Padded chest guard
Padded gloves
Padded shorts to protect upper thigh
Leg guards or pads
Kickers worn over hockey boots

◀ Hockey goalkeepers need confidence in their equipment, so they check that is fits well and is secure before training or a match.

Kit and Training

Stick skills are essential to hockey success. This player is working hard on moving the ball back and forth between a series of cones. ▶

must not handle, kick or deliberately move the ball around the pitch with any part of their body.

A hockey stick is made of wood. Sometimes it is reinforced with materials such as fibreglass or carbon fibre. Different weights and lengths exist and players try several to find out which suits them best. Every stick has a handle, shaft and a curved end which is the part that most frequently plays the ball. There are rules surrounding what players can do with the stick in a game. They must only hit the ball with the flat face of the stick and never the rounded side. They must not raise their stick in a dangerous or threatening way or hook it round their opponent's stick or foot.

Training and Practice

Hockey is a fast and skilful sport, and players must train hard so that they are fit to play a whole game. They also work hard on perfecting the various skills and techniques in the game, from passing and receiving the ball to tackling and shooting on goal. Before any major training session or match, players warm-up with jogging and other exercises and stretch the key muscles in the back, shoulders and legs.

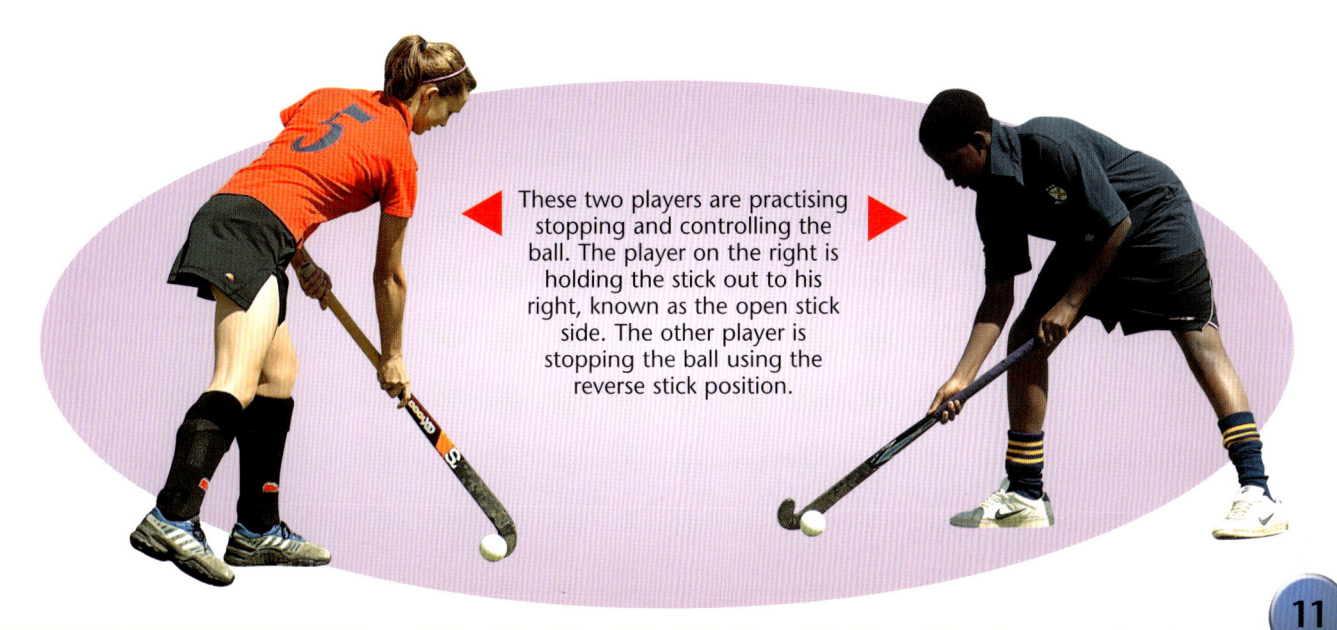

◀ These two players are practising stopping and controlling the ball. The player on the right is holding the stick out to his right, known as the open stick side. The other player is stopping the ball using the reverse stick position. ▶

11

The Push and the Hit

In hockey, as in many team ball sports, passing glues the play of the team together. Players learn to pass the ball in different ways for different situations. The two most frequently-used types of pass are the push pass and the hit. To get into the ideal position to make many passes, players require quick, nimble footwork.

Good Grip

Players usually grip near the top of the stick's handle with the left hand so that the first finger and thumb form a v-shape down the back of the stick. They hold the stick further down its shaft with their right hand. This hand offers added support and control.

The Push Pass

The most basic and common pass in

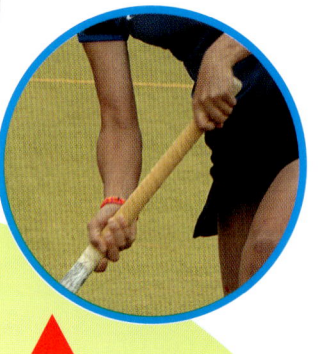

This is a good grip for playing a push pass.

The Push Pass

1 The player grips the stick with both hands about 30 centimetres apart and bends her knees to get low. She aims to start playing the ball from in front of or near her right foot. Her weight is also over her right foot.

2 The player's left shoulder should point to the pass's target and the stick should be right behind the ball. With the stick just skimming the pitch surface, the player pushes the ball, keeping the stick in contact with the ball as her body weight transfers from the right to the left foot.

3 The player aims to keep the stick on the ball for as long as possible before it travels across the pitch to a team-mate. The stick should follow through in the direction in which the ball is travelling.

The Push and the Hit

The Hit

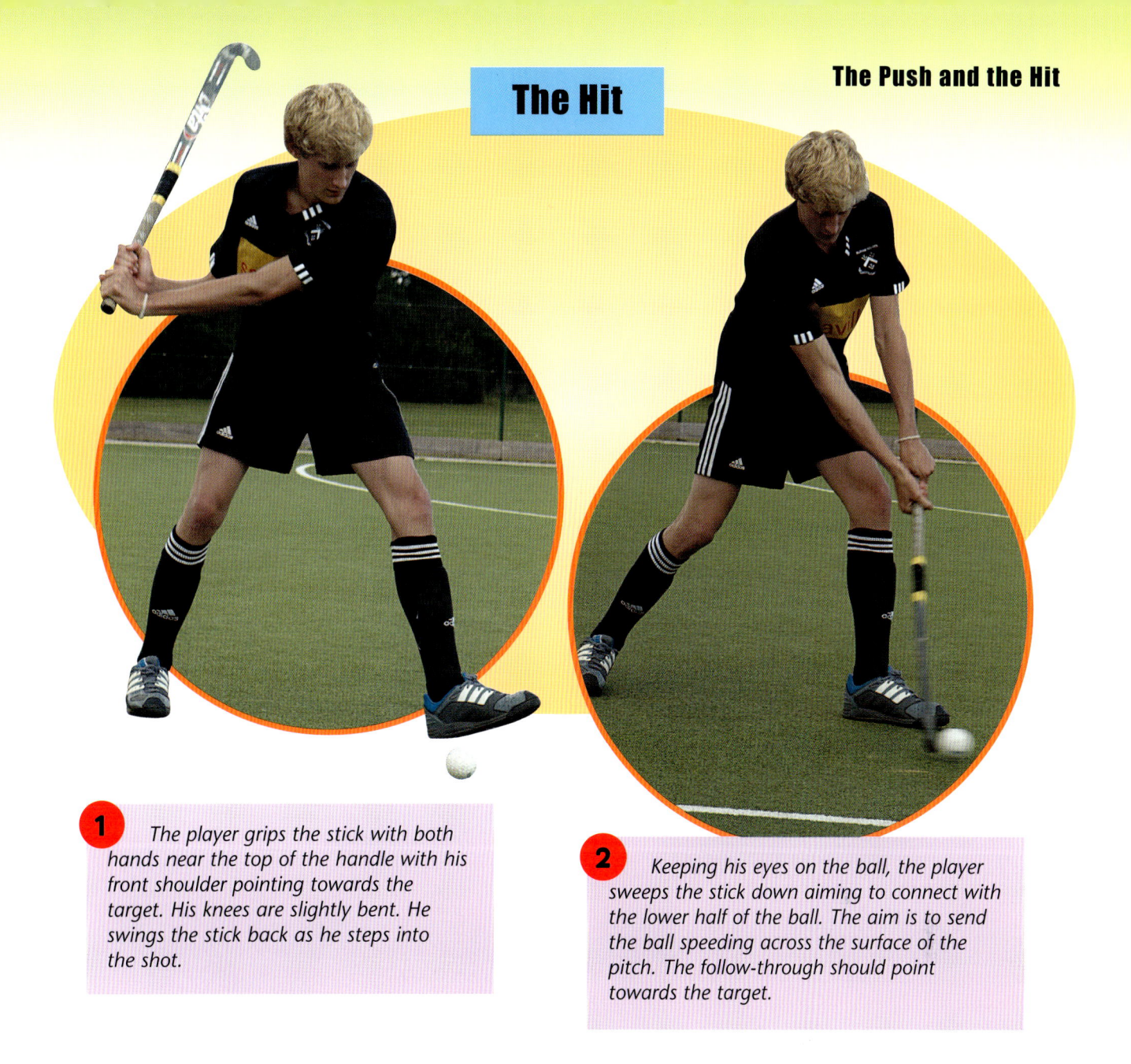

1 *The player grips the stick with both hands near the top of the handle with his front shoulder pointing towards the target. His knees are slightly bent. He swings the stick back as he steps into the shot.*

2 *Keeping his eyes on the ball, the player sweeps the stick down aiming to connect with the lower half of the ball. The aim is to send the ball speeding across the surface of the pitch. The follow-through should point towards the target.*

hockey allows a player to push the ball across the surface of the pitch. It is the best pass over shorter distances of under about 15m and can sometimes be used to make a close range shot on goal.

The Hit

The hit is a more powerful way of moving the ball in hockey and is used for long-range passes, such as 15m hits up field, and sometimes for shots on goal from the edge of the striking circle. The amount of backswing and the force of the swing down and through the ball can be altered to hit the ball with different amounts of strength known as weight.

Rubber Cubes

The earliest games of hockey were played with a square-shaped cube made of rubber instead of a ball! The first full set of rules to include a ball and the shooting circle was drawn up in 1886.

Passing and Receiving

Passing involves more than just hitting the ball. A passer has to judge the placement, timing and force of the pass. This is to prevent the ball being intercepted by an opponent and to make sure that it reaches the team-mate it is aimed for, known as the receiver, in the best way for them to control.

Good Passing
A passer has to judge where to aim the ball. When the receiver is standing still, this can be easy, but if he or she is running fast, it is trickier. The passer has to time the pass and aim the ball ahead of the receiver so that the ball and receiver will meet at the same time. Players try to keep the ball running along the surface of the pitch as this makes it easier for the receiver to control. Knowing when to pass and precisely where to position the ball is a skill that only comes with lots of practice and game time.

Receiving the Ball
Players prefer to receive the ball on their open stick side which makes it easier to

The Open Side Upright Receive

1 This receiver spots the ball coming towards him and gets his body in line with the ball's path. He will want to angle his stick forwards to stop the ball bouncing upwards.

2 He grounds his stick in front of his right foot. As the ball arrives, he keeps his stick grip relaxed so that the stick gives a little on impact to cushion the ball and slow it down.

3 With the ball under control, he turns to his right to move away with the ball on his open stick side. He can now pass or run with the ball.

14

Passing and Receiving

The Reverse Stick Stop

▶ This player receives the ball using a low reverse stick position. See how he gets so low that his knuckles almost touch the pitch.

control. A player can take the ball with their stick largely upright – from which position it is easy to move around the pitch – or if they need to reach a wider ball, may hold their stick flat and parallel to the ground. Whenever you are receiving the ball, it is vital to keep watching it and to get low by bending your knees.

The Reverse Stick Pass and Receive

Sometimes the ball is not on a player's open side. Players may need to pass or receive the ball on their reverse stick side. They do this by turning their stick with their top hand. Their bottom hand adds support. Getting low is even more crucial when receiving the ball on the reverse stick side. Players may try to control the ball with an upright reverse stick but many prefer, if there is time, to get low and get the stick to the ground.

▲ Teun de Nooijer gets ready to play a reverse push pass. His bottom hand controls the pass and generates the power to move the ball away.

Teun de Nooijer

Date of Birth: March 22nd, 1976

Nationality: Dutch

Position: Midfielder

International Caps: Over 350

Goals: 169

The outstanding Dutch player made his debut in a 1994 friendly versus New Zealand and has gone on to amass over 350 caps. An Olympic champion twice (in 1996 and 2000), the incredibly skilful de Nooijer is also the only male player to win the World Hockey Player of the Year award three times (in 2003, 2005 and 2006). In 2006, he won his sixth Champions Trophy with the Netherlands.

Moving with the Ball

Once players have the ball, they are likely to want to move with it. Their movement may be just a half turn around to face a different direction to make an immediate pass. Alternatively, they may wish to run forward into space or dribble the ball past an opponent.

Awareness and Obstruction

Good players are prepared for the ball to come at them from all angles and at different speeds. As they control the ball they already know where they would ideally like to move to next. Part of the skill here is to look up and be aware of what is happening in the game around you.

Unlike some ball sports such as football, hockey players with the ball are not allowed to shield the ball repeatedly by constantly moving their body between the ball and the defender. This will lead to an umpire signalling obstruction and usually awarding a free hit to the defender's team. A player therefore needs to keep moving or should pass the ball if a defender is close by.

Running with the Ball

Running with the ball in open play usually requires players to have their stick upright or almost upright. The left hand is at the top of the handle with the right hand a short distance below. The stick is held out in front of the player and to the right side. This allows players to move and control the ball with an open stick as they run, keeping their head up to stay aware of the game.

Luciana Aymar

Date of Birth: August 10th, 1977

Nationality: Argentinian

Position: Midfielder

International Caps: 210

Goals: 75

An attacking midfielder who made her national team debut at the 1998 World Cup, Aymar is considered one of the most skilled players in women's hockey. Her excellent control of the ball and pace has seen her average more than a goal every three games as Argentina won the 2002 World Cup and 2001 Champions Trophy.

She was voted World Hockey Player of the Year on a record three occasions (in 2001, 2004 and 2005).

Luciana Aymar looks to outsprint a New Zealand defender during a match at the 2004 Olympics.

Moving with the Ball

The Indian Dribble

1 With knees bent and hands around 30cm apart, the player pushes the ball from right to left. She then rolls her wrists and hands, twisting the stick in front of the ball using the left hand.

2 The stick guides or pushes the ball back from left to right in front of the player before the stick is turned back to its open position.

3 The stick is turned back and the move is repeated as the ball is moved back and forth in a zig-zag pattern in front of the dribbler. The stick stays close to the ball all the time.

Dribbling

Dribbling is moving with the ball controlling it with a series of small taps and nudges. Dribblers tend to bend their knees and keep the stick as close to the ball as possible. This makes it harder for a potential tackler to get the ball without hitting the dribbler's stick first and giving away a foul. Good dribblers will keep the ball on the move and may dodge and dummy to one side or the other as they dribble to try to deceive opponents.

The Indian Dribble

Named after the 1956 Indian Olympic team who amazed spectators with their skilful dribbling, in this set of moves the stick is switched repeatedly from open to reverse stick side to control the ball.

17

Attacking

Attacking occurs when the players in the team with possession and control of the ball move forward. The whole aim of attacking is to get the ball into the other team's shooting circle and in the control of a team-mate who is in a position to shoot.

Teamwork and Individual Play

Players use a mixture of short passing, long passing and running and dribbling to manoeuvre the ball into threatening positions. A ball can be hit and passed up and around the pitch faster than one player can run with it, so swift, accurate passing is usually used to surge forward. On occasion, though, a piece of individual skill such as a player dribbling past one or two defenders may lead to a goalscoring chance. Even individual attacking may involve team-mates. For example, one attacker may make a decoy run which draws one or more defenders away. This may create space for the attacker with the ball to run into.

The Dummy and Drag

1 In this dummy and drag move the attacker leans and moves to her right. She needs to convince the defender that she intends to head in that direction.

2 As the defender shifts her bodyweight to cover the attacker's move to the right, the attacker drags the ball sharply to her left ready to sprint away with the ball under control.

Attacking

The One-Two Pass

1 The attacker on the left makes a quick push pass to her team-mate. She then starts sprinting past the defender (in red).

2 The receiver collects the ball and passes back to her team-mate behind the defender. The defender is cut out by this one-two pass.

Attacking Space

Attackers need to spot space in threatening areas which their team-mate with the ball can reach with a pass. They must attack the space, getting free of any defenders and timing their run well so they can receive a pass. Sometimes, this may involve a forward sprinting towards the sideline to receive a long ball hit by a defender or midfielder. Similarly, an attacker may make an overlapping run down the line free of a defender to receive a pass from a team-mate. On other occasions, more intricate team play may result in a series of short passes before a through ball is played carefully behind defenders for an attacker to run on to.

Disguise and Deception

With most players preferring to move the ball on their open stick side, the defending team can sometimes predict where the ball may head next and put in a tackle or gain an interception (see page 23). To counter this, the attacking players try to use various ways to deceive their opponents or disguise their intent. These include decoy runs, dummy moves (such as pretending to run in one direction but actually running in another) and generally, trying to disguise what type of pass they intend to make.

Shooting and Defending

Without accurate shooting, a team's dominance in a game cannot be turned into crucial goals. An attacker's first thought once inside the striking circle with the ball should be to shoot. Only if the angle or the position makes it hard or impossible to get a shot on target should the attacker look instead for a good pass to a team-mate.

Quick Shooting

Good shooters decide in a split-second where to target their shot and what sort of stroke to use. If they have time and are at the edge of the striking circle, players often use a hit for maximum power. Closer in, the ball can be hit with a push, slap or reverse stick pass or hit. Shooters may have to react to the ball coming suddenly to them. In all cases, shooters strive to get the ball on target and to follow up their shot. Many goals are scored at the second attempt after a saved ball rebounds out.

The Slap Shot

1 She grips the stick with her hands apart and has a similar stance to the push pass, side-on to the ball. Her weight is ideally over the back foot. She draws back the stick some distance behind the ball.

2 She brings the stick forward sharply with a sweeping movement with the bottom of the stick grazing the ground. The ball is carried along with the sweeping movement and released as she transfers her weight from the back to the front leg.

Shooting and Defending

Alyson Annan
Date of Birth: June 21st, 1973
Nationality: Australian
Position: Attacker
International Caps: 228
Goals: 166

Alyson Annan was a powerful attacker in the 1990s and possessed one of the hardest shots in women's hockey. Her heavy scoring helped Australia to become the dominant side of the decade, winning two Olympic gold medals and four Champions Trophies. Annan won the World Hockey Player of the Year award twice (1998 and 2000) and retired in 2003, becoming a coach in the Netherlands.

◀ Alyson Annan gets low to drive the ball forward. Her eyes stay on the ball throughout the stroke.

The Slap Shot
A cross between the hit and the push pass, a slap shot is often used for shooting, particularly when a sudden chance occurs or from close range. The slap shot can be played quickly and with some power.

Defending
Defenders work hard to stop their opponents getting into a position to shoot and try to regain the ball for their team. To do this they can tackle or try to intercept the ball (see page 23), block passes or shots and mark opponents. Most marking is player-to-player. It involves defenders keeping close to their opponent, usually between the opponent and their own goal, and moving as they do. The aim of marking is to reduce the opportunities for the opponent to receive the ball.

◀ The defender (in red) closes down an attacker with the ball, keeping goalside of him and looking for a chance to challenge for the ball.

Intercepting and Tackling

There are three main ways to regain the ball. The first is when an opponent makes an unforced mistake and loses control of the ball or knocks the ball out of play. The second is when a defender intercepts an opposing team member's pass and the third is tackling – a direct challenge for the ball when it is in the control of an opponent.

Block Tackles

Block tackles are firm tackles usually made with both the tackler's hands on the stick. The most common block tackle and often the most secure is made on the open stick side when the tackled player is on the tackler's right. A more difficult block tackle can also be made on the reverse stick side when the tackled player is to the left. With all tackles, it is vital to be strong, well-balanced and decisive. Watch the ball not the player and time your tackle so that you do not hit your opponent's body or stick, as this would count as a foul.

The Open Side Block Tackle

1 *A tackler closes in to make a tackle on an opponent. He steps into the tackle with his left foot and gets low, with his stick on or just above the ground to act as a solid barrier.*

2 *The tackle is made firmly with the stick face angled towards the ball which is dislodged from the opponent's control. The tackler's right foot can be pivoted on if he needs to change his angle.*

Intercepting and Tackling

The Jab Tackle

1 *The player holds her stick with both hands, with the handle pointing towards her waist and her left foot forward. She watches the ball, waiting for the best moment, such as when the ball leaves the opponent's stick.*

2 *She jabs the stick forward with a thrust of the body and lunge of the left hand. The tackler aims to strike the ball out of the path and control of her opponent. With the ball dislodged, she must react quickly to collect and control the ball.*

Jab Tackles

The jab tackle relies on speed and timing to lunge the stick at the ball to knock it out of the control of the opponent. Sometimes, a tackler fakes a jab tackle to unbalance the opponent before attempting a real jab or block tackle.

Interceptions

Interceptions are made when a member of the defending team latches on to or cuts out a pass made by an opponent. Interceptions need timing and good judgement and can lead to the ball being regained without a tackle.

This player has stayed alert and has spotted a weak pass made by an opponent. Judging that she can reach it first, she sprints forward, lunging in the reverse stick position to intercept the ball and cut out the pass.

The Penalty Corner

A long corner is awarded when the ball travels over the backline of the pitch and was touched last by a defender unintentionally. If the defender deliberately takes the ball over the backline then a penalty corner is given. Also awarded for a range of fouls, a penalty corner is an excellent chance for a team to score a goal.

Taking a Penalty Corner

When a penalty corner is awarded, over half of the defending team must retreat to behind the halfway line. A maximum of five defenders including the goalkeeper can position themselves, their feet and sticks behind the backline. All the attackers must stand outside the striking circle until the ball is pushed out by their team-mate from the backline and at least 10m away from the goal.

Sohail Abbas follows-through powerfully as he completes a penalty corner shot on goal. The Pakistan player was one of the most successful penalty corner takers in international hockey.

Sohail Abbas

Date of Birth: June 9th, 1977

Nationality: Pakistani

Position: Defender

International caps: 250

Goals: 288

Abbas began his hockey career as an attacker but moved back into defence. His impact on world hockey came through his mastery of the drag flick, a powerful method of powering the ball towards the goal. Becoming an absolutely lethal penalty corner striker, Abbas scored a record 274 international goals for Pakistan. He retired from international hockey at the end of 2004 but continued playing in the professional league in the Netherlands.

The Penalty Corner

Penalty Corner Tactics

Teams practise their penalty corner moves frequently. The aim is to perfect their play so that a penalty corner results in their striker being able to take a direct shot on goal. If the pass out is not well directed or is slow, or if the defenders are especially quick off the line, this may not be possible. So teams work on alternative moves, including quick passes to attackers to either side who may have a better angle and more space to take shot on goal. Attackers also follow up in the hope of a rebound off a defender's stick, the goalkeeper or the goal.

The Penalty Corner

1 The penalty corner begins with the player pushing or hitting the ball out from the backline. She makes sure that one of her feet is behind the backline and aims for a point, agreed with her team-mates, outside the circle.

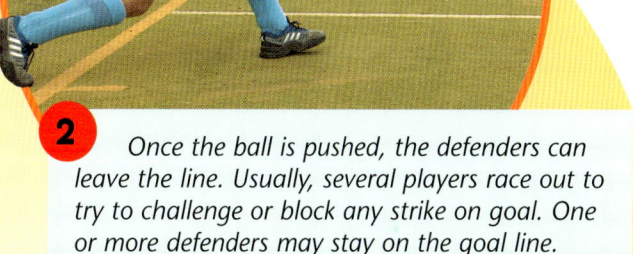

2 Once the ball is pushed, the defenders can leave the line. Usually, several players race out to try to challenge or block any strike on goal. One or more defenders may stay on the goal line.

3 The ball must travel outside the circle but, following rule changes, it no longer has to be stopped still by the attacking team. Some teams still choose to employ a player to trap the ball, but often the strikers will control the ball themselves.

4 The penalty striker is allowed to hit, push or flick the ball towards the goal. If the ball is hit, it must remain under 460mm high (the height of the backboard) to be a goal, unless it is deflected higher off an opponent's stick or body.

25

Goalkeeping and Penalties

The goalkeeper is the last line of defence. Goalkeepers aim to stop goals and they can do this with almost any part of their body, which is why they are so heavily padded and protected. Goalkeepers have a good view of the play ahead and should command their circle, communicating with and organizing their team-mates to form a strong defence.

Shot Saving

The majority of shots that threaten a goal come in at a low height. This means that goalkeepers need quick footwork to be able to get their feet and body in line with the ball to block it using their pads and feet. Then, they must clear it either using their feet or, if they have more time on the ball, their stick. Some shots may come through at a greater height. Keepers can use their stick, or ideally, their hands to stop the ball, but must not catch it. Instead, they cushion

The Block and Clear

1 This keeper is in a good ready stance, balanced and ready to move in any direction as a shot comes in. As the shot comes in she starts to get her pads together and in line with the ball to block the shot.

2 After the ball drops to the floor, the goalkeeper turns her body and kicks the ball away from danger. The kick is made firmly with her bodyweight over the ball. A kick out to the sideline is far safer than kicking straight back up the pitch.

Goalkeeping and Penalties

This keeper makes a diving save. Her body and pads face the ball's direction and the stick is stretched out to make the stop.

The penalty taker stands within playing distance of the ball and waits for the umpire's whistle before making an attempt on goal. The goalkeeper is in the ready position but can only start to dive when the ball has been played.

the ball's impact and once the ball has dropped to the ground clear it with their feet or stick.

One-on-Ones
Sometimes, an opponent bursts through with the ball, forcing a one-on-one situation with the goalkeeper. If keepers stay on their line, they offer more of the goal for the attacker to aim at. They may choose to come off their line towards the attacker to narrow the angle and give their opponent less of the goal to shoot at. This run has to be well-judged, otherwise the attacker may round the keeper or pass to a free team-mate to score.

Penalty Strokes
An umpire awards a penalty stroke when a serious offence occurs inside the shooting circle, such as when a player commits a dangerous foul or illegally stops a likely goal. The ball is placed on the penalty spot in front of the goal and all players except the penalty taker and the goalkeeper must be outside the 25m line. The penalty taker is allowed to push, scoop or flick the ball towards goal but may not hit or drag-flick the ball. A penalty stroke is an excellent chance to score, but many goalkeepers manage to make a save. The penalty striker cannot take a second shot off the rebound and the stroke is said to be over if the ball becomes caught up in the goalkeeper's equipment or leaves the shooting circle.

Statistics and Records

Olympic Winners

Men
1908 Great Britain
1920 Great Britain
1928 India
1932 India
1936 India
1948 India
1952 India
1956 India
1960 Pakistan
1964 India
1968 Pakistan
1972 West Germany
1976 New Zealand
1980 India
1984 Pakistan
1988 Great Britain
1992 Germany
1996 Netherlands
2000 Netherlands
2004 Australia

Women
1980 Zimbabwe
1984 Netherlands
1988 Australia
1992 Spain
1996 Australia
2000 Australia
2004 Germany

Hockey World Cup Winners

Men
1971 Pakistan
1973 Netherlands
1975 India
1978 Pakistan
1982 Pakistan
1986 Australia
1990 Netherlands
1994 Pakistan
1998 Netherlands
2002 Germany
2006 Germany

Women
1974 Netherlands
1976 West Germany
1978 Netherlands
1981 West Germany
1983 Netherlands
1986 Netherlands
1990 Netherlands
1994 Australia
1998 Australia
2002 Argentina
2006 Netherlands

Champions Trophy Finalists

Men

Country	Winner	Runner-up
Australia	8	9
Germany	8	6
Netherlands	8	5
Pakistan	3 6	
Spain	1	0
Great Britain	0	1
Korea	0	1

Women

Country	Winner	Runner-up
Australia	6	3
Netherlands	5	3
Germany	1	4
Argentina	1	2
China	1	2
Korea	1	1

Biggest International Win

Men
Argentina 30 Dominican Republic 0 (2003 Pan-Am Games)

Women
Argentina 26 Peru 0 (2003 Pan-Am Games)

Most Successful Captain

Stephan Veen of the Netherlands is the only player to have won the three major tournaments whilst captain – the 1998 World Cup, the 2000 Champions Trophy and the 2000 Olympics.

Most International Goals

Men
Sohall Abbas (Pakistan) 288 goals in 240 matches

Women
Natella Krasnikova (Russia) 220 goals in 173 matches

Most International Matches

Men
Jeroen Delmee (Netherlands) 351 matches

Women
Karen Brown (England) 355 matches

Glossary

Backboard A 460mm-high solid piece of material, usually wood, running along the back of the goal.

Backline The line marking the end of a hockey pitch. It is known as the goal line when it runs between the two goal posts.

Dribble The movement of a player while controlling the ball with the stick.

Free hit A penalty awarded only when a player or team has been disadvantaged by an opponent breaking the rules. They can only be awarded for offences outside the shooting circle.

Goalside When a player is positioned between their own goal and an opponent or between their goal and the ball.

Hit-in A way of restarting play from the sideline after the ball has gone out of play.

Kickers The name given to the boots worn by a hockey goalkeeper.

Long corner A way of restarting play after the ball is played accidentally by the defending team over the backline.

Marking Standing close to an opponent and guarding them whilst the other team attacks.

Open stick When the stick is turned so that its flat side (the blade) faces to the left.

Penalty stroke A penalty awarded to an attacker taken from the penalty spot with only the goalkeeper to defend the stroke.

Reverse stick When the stick is turned so that the 'toe' or end of the stick points down and the flat side of the stick faces right.

Shooting circle The D-shaped area surrounding each goal inside which teams can try to score a goal.

Sin-bin An area or bench outside the pitch where players who have been shown a yellow card must stay until they are allowed back on the pitch.

Websites

www.fihockey.org
The website of the International Hockey Federation (FIH), the organization which runs world hockey. The latest rules of the game can be downloaded from the website.

www.englandhockey.co.uk
The homepage of England Hockey, including news, results and fixtures and downloadable free magazines.

www.scottish-hockey.org.uk
The official Scottish Hockey website, with details of fixtures, youth camps and clubs in Scotland.

www.welsh-hockey.co.uk
The homepage of the Welsh Hockey Union, which contains tournament news and a handy list of links to hockey throughout the United Kingdom.

www.hockey.org.au
The website of the organizers of hockey in Australia.

www.planetfieldhockey.com
One of the best sites on the Web for hockey-related interviews, features and coaching tips.

Note to parents and teachers: every effort has been made by the Publishers to ensure that these websites are suitable for children, that they are of the highest educational value, and that they contain no inappropriate or offensive material. However, because of the nature of the Internet, it is impossible to guarantee that the contents of these sites will not be altered. We strongly advise that Internet access is supervised by a responsible adult.

Index

Abbas, Sohail 24, 28
Annan, Alyson 21
attacking 18–19
awareness 16
Aymar, Luciana 16

backboards 8, 29
backline 8, 29
ball 10–11
block and clear 26
block tackles 22
boots 10
Brown, Karen 28

centre circle 8

De Nooijer, Teun 15
defending 21
Delmee, Jeroen 28
disguise and deception 19
dribbling 17, 29
dummy and drag 18

fouls 9, 27
free hits 9, 16, 29

game 6
goal line 8
goal scoring 6
goalkeepers 6, 10, 26–7
goals 8
goalside 29
grip 12

hand signals 9
helmets 10

history 7, 13
hit-ins 8–9, 29
hits 13, 20

in and out of play 8–9
Indian dribble 17
interceptions 23

jab tackles 23

kickers 10, 29
kit 10
Krasnikova, Natella 28

long corners 8, 9, 24, 29

marking 21, 29
mini hockey 7
mouthguards 10
moving with the ball 16–17

obstruction 16
Olympic Games 6–7, 28
one-on-ones 27
one-two pass 19
open side block tackles 22
open side upright receive 14
open stick 11, 29

passing 12–13, 14
penalty corners 9, 24–5
penalty spot 8, 27
penalty strokes 27, 29
pitch 8
push pass 12–13
pushback 6

receiving 14–15
reverse stick 11, 15, 29
reverse stick stop 15
rules 6, 9, 10–11, 16, 24, 27
running with the ball 16

shinguards 10
shooting 20–1
shooting circles 6, 8, 29
shot saving 26–7
sin-bin 9, 29
slap shot 20–1
stick use 6
sticks 11
substitutes 10

tackling 22–3
teams 10
teamwork 18–19
three card system 9
tournaments 6–7
training and practice 11

umpires 9

Veen, Stephan 28

warming up 11

30